Eek, Sheep!

Written by Danny Pearson

Illustrated by Steve May

Collins

1 Woolly army

Sixty hungry, grumpy sheep stood on the stormy hill.

The wind was wild, and rain splashed around the soggy sheep.

One sheep leader stepped out in front and gazed into the distance. "Let's go to town. March on, brave flock!" she cried.

The hungry woolly army went on the march.
The ground beneath their hooves was muddy.

The flock shuffled down the slippery hill.

The cheeky sheep didn't stop until they reached a campsite.

"Eek, sheep!" a worried man cried.

They took mangoes, potatoes and sticky honey.
Next, the hungry sheep marched into town.

2 The town

The greedy flock were keen to take over the town.

The ground shook.

"Eek, sheep!" a lady cried.

The hungry sheep headed for the middle
of the town.

The sheep rampaged into the market. They found the cheese stand.

The rude sheep disrupted a film show next.

Philippa stood up.

"Why are there sheep in here?" she howled.

The woolly army were reckless.

But the sheep were still hungry! The fleecy army got to the local school. They found fruit juice and cookies.

"Eek, sheep!" a boy cried.

The cheeky sheep had noodles on a rowing boat.

Philippa had to swerve. A sheep was pushing a trolley full of cheese and fizzy ginger pop.

Philippa was annoyed. "Look out!"

"Follow me!" Philippa cried. "I have jelly."
Sheep love wobbly jelly. The jelly was bait.

Philippa threw the jelly into the local
fish and chip shop. Greedily, the sheep followed
the jelly. It was a trap.

The sixty sheep were stuck. They were too woolly!

"I can help you," said Philippa. "Now, apologise and stop your rampage."

The sheep were sorry.

3 Woolly jumpers

"Luckily my mum is a farmer," said Philippa.
"Time to make a jumper or two."

"I have the power," cried Philippa.

19

Philippa went quickly into the shop.

Time for a shave.

buzz

The sheep were now free! Philippa was queen of the sheep.

"Tomorrow we will celebrate with a party!" somebody cried. "We can live in peace again."

Philippa made sparkly rainbow jumpers from the wool. The happy sheep had a woolly jumper parade to celebrate.

Sheep spotting

Go back and find these sheep from the woolly army.

A real rampage

This greedy woolly army of goats took over a town in Wales! These goats inspired the story.

The fleecy army

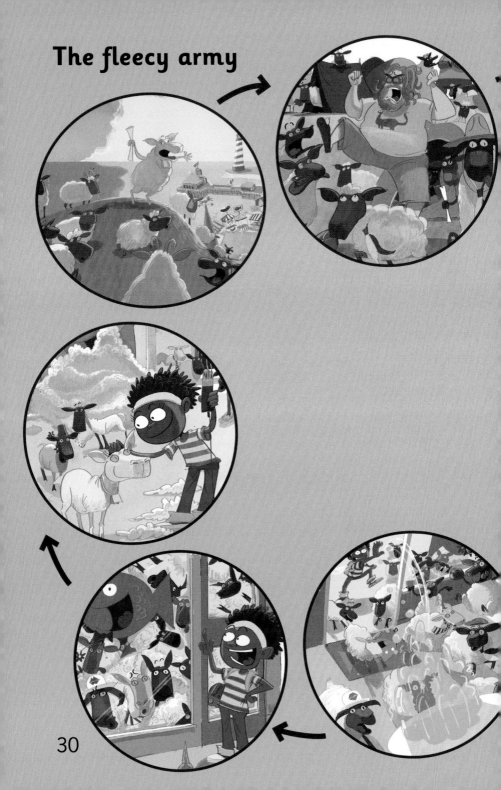

🐾 Review: After reading 🐾

Use your assessment from hearing the children read to choose any GPCs, words or tricky words that need additional practice.

Read 1: Decoding

- Turn to page 9 and point to the word **headed**. Ask the children to read the whole sentence then suggest a phrase with a similar meaning to **headed**. (e.g. *move towards, make for*)
- Help the children to get quicker at reading multi-syllable words. Ask them to use the chunking method to read each syllable in these words:
  ram/paged   **po/ta/toes**   **a/pol/o/gise**   **cel/e/brate**
- Challenge the children to take turns to read a page fluently. Say: Can you blend in your head when you read less familiar words?

Read 2: Prosody

- Model reading page 12 in a storyteller voice, emphasising the excitement and humour.
- Ask the children to work in small groups to prepare a dramatic reading of pages 12 and 13. Suggest they think about different voices for the characters, the narrative and sound words. Say: Think about pace and tone, too.
- Encourage groups of children to read the pages. Discuss how they made the story sound funny and exciting.

Read 3: Comprehension

- Ask the children if they have read any funny stories about sheep or other farm animals. Ask: What happened? Why was it funny?
- Use pages 30 and 31 to discuss the stages of the story and to identify the turning point. How did Philippa stop the sheep? Remind the children that the jelly was called **bait**. Ask: Why was jelly bait? (e.g. *Philippa used it to draw the sheep into a trap because they loved the jelly*)
- Focus on how the language makes the story funny.
  - o On page 3, discuss how the sheep's words aren't like a sheep's at all.
  - o On page 5, discuss the word **shuffled**. Ask: Can you imagine a sheep **shuffling**? Ask the children to mime a shuffling sheep.
  - o Discuss the repetition of **Eek, sheep!** Ask: In what ways are the people's reactions funny? (e.g. *on pages 12 and 13, they are exaggerated, hysterical*)
- Bonus content: Challenge the children to make up a story similar to *Eek, Sheep!* but with the goats on pages 28 and 29 as the main characters. They could follow the same route as the sheep's (pages 26 and 27). Ask: What do the goats want? What happens in each spot?